Potty Training In One Week

Gina Ford

LONDON

7 9 10 8

Copyright © Gina Ford 2003

Gina Ford has asserted her moral right to be identified as the author of this
work in accordance with the Copyright, Designs and Patents Act 1988.

First published in the United Kingdom in 2003 by Vermilion

This edition published in the United Kingdom in 2006
by Vermilion, an imprint of Ebury Publishing
Random House UK Ltd
Random House · 20 Vauxhall Bridge Road · London SW1V 2SA

Random House Australia (Pty) Limited
20 Alfred Street · Milsons Point · Sydney · New South Wales 2061 · Australia

Random House New Zealand Limited
18 Poland Road · Glenfield · Auckland 10 · New Zealand

Random House (Pty) Limited
Isle of Houghton · Corner of Boundary Road & Carse O'Gowrie
Houghton 2198 · South Africa

Random House Publishers India Private Limited
301 World Trade Tower · Hotel Intercontinental Grand Complex
Barakhamba Lane · New Delhi 110 001 · India

Random House UK Limited Reg. No. 954009
www.randomhouse.co.uk

Papers used by Vermilion are natural, recyclable products made from
wood grown in sustainable forests.

A CIP catalogue record for this book is available from the British Library

ISBN 9780091912734 (from January 2007)
ISBN 0091912733

Text design by Lovelock & Co.
Printed and bound in Great Britain by Mackays of Chatham plc · Chatham · Kent

Contents

First Things First

Introduction

Like every other aspect of child care the advice given by experts on what age it is best to attempt potty training a child is deeply divided. This makes it very difficult for parents to judge whether their child is ready to give up nappies. Many care experts advise that the children should be left to decide when they are ready to come out of nappies. Others reckon that it is best to start putting a baby on the pot at regular intervals each day from as young as nine months. Nanny Smith advises that parents use a muslin nappy to tie their baby to spars of the playpen to support them while sitting on the pot. While these approaches may work for some children some of the time, none will work for all children all of the time. The main reason being that the key to successful potty training is not just about whether your child is ready to be potty trained but whether the parents and the rest of the family are ready. Even if a child is showing all the signs of being ready to give up nappies, potty training can end up in disaster if the parents are not ready. If followed to the letter my programme for potty training usually works within a week and avoids many of the usual pit-falls encountered by parents when potty training. As with all the other advice I give parents on baby and child care my opinions are formed from hands-on experience, actually working with a vast number of parents and their children.

What is potty training?

I believe that a child who has been successfully potty trained will know when he needs to use the potty or toilet and be capable of going to the potty or toilet by himself, pulling his pants down without assistance then using the potty or toilet and pulling his pants back up and washing and drying his hands. A child who has constantly to be reminded to use the potty and needs assistance with his clothes is in my opinion not truly potty trained. None of these tasks can be achieved until the child is able to control his bowel and bladder movements. The age at which this happens varies very much from child to child and attempting to start before the child has bladder control will certainly lead to many accidents and much frustration for both the child and the parents.

When to start

Parents frequently ask me what is the best age to start potty training. While all children are different, in my experience of working with hundreds of mothers and children, the majority are ready to be trained somewhere between the ages of 18 and 24 months. Before 18 months, very few children's muscles are developed enough for the bladder control necessary for potty training. While we have all heard the stories from our mothers, aunties and grandmas, how in their day the baby was potty trained by the age of one year, the reality is that it was really the mother who was trained and not the baby. By sitting the baby on the potty at frequent times during the day she would, more often than not catch the urine or the bowel movement. While this obviously saved her the laborious task of washing and sterilizing the terry nappies used in those days, the baby could not be called potty trained in the true sense. I cannot stress too strongly that a toddler who is truly potty trained will recognise when he needs to pass urine or have a bowel movement and be capable of going to his potty, pulling down his own pants, and using the potty before pulling his pants up again. Often a child may be aware when he needs to do a pee or a poo but if he has not learned to dress and undress himself potty training could prove very difficult.

Signs to watch for

Once your toddler reaches 18 months there are signs to watch
out for that indicate he may be ready for Stage One of preparing
for potty training. There are also certain levels of ability which
your child should have reached to ensure successful potty
training.

These important signs and levels of ability that will indicate if
your toddler is ready to potty train are:

1   He is over 18 months of age.
2   His nappy is frequently dry when you get him up from his
     lunchtime nap. A dry nappy a couple of hours since his
     last nappy change would also be an indication that he is
     getting some bladder control.

  Potty Training in One Week

3   He is aware when he is doing a poo, i.e. going very quiet
    and showing signs of concentration, or points to his nappy
    and says poo or pee pee when he has done one.

4   He can understand and follow simple instructions, i.e. go
    and fetch your red ball or put your toy in the box.

5   He is eager to participate in taking off his own clothes, i.e.
    shoes, socks and shorts, and understands what pulling his
    shorts up and down mean.

6   Can point to the different parts of his body when you name
    them, for example 'where's your tummy button?' or
    'where's your nose?' etc.

7   He has the ability to sit still and occupy himself or
    concentrate for five to ten minutes with a toy, book or
    watching a video.

If your child were not showing all of the signs listed above I
would not attempt Stage One. Even if his nappy is frequently dry

after a couple of hours, it would be very difficult to train him if he was unable to sit still for more than a few minutes at a time, or does not obey simple requests. It would be advisable to work on his ability and wait for the right moment before attempting Stage One. Remember that the key to potty training quickly and successfully is to start when the child and parents are ready.

Encouraging co-operation

If you are having trouble encouraging your child to participate in tasks such as dressing and undressing and helping to tidy his toys away I would suggest introducing a star chart. Then when he willingly co-operates with one of these tasks I would reward him with lots of praise and a star or sticker. Even if he doesn't fully understand the concept of the star chart, the number of stars or stickers each day on the chart will be a good indicator as to how co-operative he has been.

I also find it helpful to mark a cross in the box every time I request the child to do something and if they co-operate I cover the cross with a sticker. You can then tell at a glance how many of your requests he has completed willingly. Once you see several consecutive days where nearly all the crosses are covered with a sticker, and your child is showing all the other signs of being ready for potty training, I would try Stage One.

Mark

aged 4 years

Mark was three years and nine months when I went to care for his baby sister. His mother had tried potty training him on two occasions, the first time when he was just over two years and the second time when he was two and a half years. Each time it had ended in disaster with Mark throwing mega tantrums when his mother tried to persuade him to go on the potty. The health visitor advised Mark's mother against trying again and to wait until Mark took the initiative himself. She assured Mark's mother that by the time he got to four years of age he would automatically want to abandon his nappies of his own free will.

While I think that is possibly true for most children, there are always a few very stubborn ones who despite reaching an age of being fully aware that they need to use the loo, will constantly resist going into pants. Mark certainly fell into that category. During my first few weeks I observed that every request his parents made was met with whining or tantrums.

Getting dressed in the morning was a nightmare, his mother would usually start off by cajoling and bribing Mark to get dressed, the whole fiasco often taking as long as forty minutes to get him into his clothes. But, more often than not Mark would end up hysterical, with lots of tears and tantrums, as his mother would physically hold him down to get him dressed. The same performance would be repeated at bedtime. Mealtimes were another time which were very fraught. His mother forever worried that he was not eating enough, would end up spoon-feeding him and bribing him with the reward of sweets and ice-creams if he finished his meal.

By the time Mark reached four years of age his mother asked

if I thought that he was ready to start potty training. I gave my honest opinion that I felt that until Mark had learned to take instruction regarding the basic things in his life, like getting dressed, tidying his toys away, eating etc., it would be highly unlikely that he would be willing to follow even the first basic stages of potty training. I advised his parents that we sit down and make a list of basic rules to follow when dealing with Mark's difficult behaviour. Once we had cracked the problem of his day-to-day behaviour I was sure that he would potty train very quickly.

The first thing I did was to draw up a star chart for which Mark was to be given a star each time he co-operated with the three things listed on the chart. The first was that he ate at least most of his meal nicely, and without assistance from either of his parents. The second was that he dressed himself, and the third was that he tidied his toys away when requested. We explained to Mark that if he got four stars in his box each day, he could then choose four sweets from the treat jar at the end of the day after he had had his tea. The first few days were very fraught. Mark would throw tantrum after tantrum at mealtimes and would throw his clothes all over the room when we requested he got dressed. I explained to his mother that it was very important that we dealt with these tantrums very calmly and very consistently. If he didn't want to eat, we were to say, 'that's fine, you're obviously not hungry' and take the food away, making no further comment. If he asked for food an hour or two later he was not to be given it until either the allocated snack time or mealtime.

With his dressing he was to be left alone in his room with his clothes and told that once he was dressed we would all go to the swing park. We would return to the room every two or three minutes to remind him that once he was dressed we would all go to the park, but on no account was he to be helped with dressing. When he refused to tidy his toys away, we simply took the toys away that he had been playing with and told him that he would get them back the following day, if he had decided that he wanted to look after them properly.

The first two days were an absolute nightmare, with toys and clothes being thrown everywhere, and on one occasion it took up to two hours for him to get dressed. During breakfast and lunch much of the meal would end up on the floor or in the bin. While we stood firm on the rules that were set, we never showed any frustration or anger towards his behaviour – which at times was very difficult. We reassured him that when he was a good boy he would get a star, and four stars would mean a treat.

Things took a turn for the better on the third day when he managed to got three stars on his chart. Unknown to him I secretly stuck on a fourth star so that he could get his reward that night. Nearly three days without sweets, treats and videos meant he was over the moon at being rewarded for his good behaviour. We made quite a lot of fuss over him about how clever he was and how proud we were of him, also how proud daddy, granny and auntie etc. was of him.

By the end of the week Mark was like a different child. He dressed himself, ate his meals and tidied his toys away without any fuss or assistance. I felt that he was now ready to be potty trained and because of his age I suggested that we go straight into the second stage of potty training. On the Monday of the following week we put an extra line on his star chart and explained that he was a big boy now and could wear big boy pants like daddy, and that he should do his pee or poo in the potty or loo.

Each time he managed this he would be given a special gold star, and if he got four gold stars a day he would be given either a small ice-cream or jelly after his tea. Although he had quite a few accidents the first couple of days he always managed to get at least four stars on his chart. By the fourth day Mark was completely dry during the day and happily using the big loo most of the time.

We continued to use nappies at night for a further three

months, by which time he was waking up dry most mornings. We installed a potty and a night light in his bedroom at this stage explaining that should he need a pee in the night he should get up and use the potty. The first few nights we had a couple of accidents, one in the bed and another one when he accidentally missed the potty. After that he was totally dry every morning.

Preparation for Potty Training

What you need

Before you begin to prepare your child for potty training make sure that you have all the right equipment. It is essential to have two potties; one for upstairs and one for downstairs as it saves having to transfer it up and down stairs. Remember that during the early stages of training it is often a case of getting the potty to the child, rather than the child to the potty.

Two potties – These should be a simple sturdy design with a wide brim and a splashguard at the front, and an extra wide base so the potty stays on the floor when your child stands up. Avoid fancy or complicated designs with lids at this stage. I also would suggest that it is better to choose two potties of the same design and colour. I have been caught out on several occasions when a toddler refuses to do a pee in the green potty downstairs because he wants to do it in the red one upstairs!

Child's toilet seat – This is a specially designed seat that fits inside the toilet seat. Choose one that is well padded, and with handles at each side which the child can hold onto to keep himself steady.

Cushion – Until your toddler is properly trained it is advisable to take precautions when travelling in the car, or using the buggy. I would advise buying a thin cushion pad and cover it with a polythene bag. This can then be covered with a removable washable, decorative cover. It can be your child's special cushion and used in the buggy, car seat or when visiting friends, and safer than just placing a plastic bag on the seat. I have found that when a plastic bag is placed on a seat, the child often sees it as a safety net, and is less inclined to mention he needs to pee. He is unaware his cushion has a plastic cover, and because it is his special cushion he will be more likely to want to keep it dry.

Eight pairs of pants – It is important to buy them a couple of sizes bigger thus making it easier for your child to pull them up and down by himself. Also allowing for shrinkage due to washing and drying. I never advise using pull-up nappies, as once the nappy is off it should stay off and only be replaced for sleep times. Pull-ups give confusing messages to toddlers and so I wouldn't use them.

Selection of storybooks, cassette tapes and videos – Buy or borrow from your local library a selection of short story books and nursery rhyme tapes so he is less likely to become bored while on the potty. Video some suitable children's programmes, which can be used as a last resort if he becomes stubborn about using the potty.

Star chart – Design a brightly coloured star chart with his name on it, and buy lots of different coloured stars in assorted sizes. When he has successfully used the potty several times in a row, give him an extra big star for being so clever.

Face cloths – It is easier for a small child to dry his hands himself on a small face cloth rather than a towel. Choose several with his favourite cartoon characters on to encourage hand-washing after using the potty.

Booster step – This is a small step for your child to stand on, enabling him to reach the basin easily when washing his hands. Eventually this can be used for getting up onto the toilet.

Clothing – For the first few days of potty training it is best to dress your child in a short t-shirt that does not need to be pulled up above the pants. Furthermore, once the training is under way and going well make sure you dress him in clothes that he finds quick and easy when he uses the potty.

For example vests that fasten under legs should be changed to ordinary ones and avoid dungarees and trousers with lots of buttons and belts. Until he is trained it is better to go for simple shorts or tracksuit-type bottoms with a t-shirt or sweat shirt.

Two buckets – These are for use once you have begun Stage One and stopped using nappies. One is filled with warm water and disinfectant to clean up any misses. The other is filled with cold-water soap powder solution to drop wet or soiled pants into.

Potty Training in One Week

Introducing the potty

If you wait until your child is 18 months or older and showing all the signs and levels of ability he will be much more likely to understand what the potty is for when it is explained to him. Many experts advise introducing the potty long before the child is ready to be potty trained, so that they become familiar with it. In my experience most young children have a very low boredom threshold and in houses where the potty was introduced long before it was needed only led to the child seeing it as a toy for filling up with bricks and the like. Therefore I suggest that you wait until the child is showing all the signs of readiness listed on page 12, before putting a potty in the bathroom upstairs and one in the toilet downstairs.

As all children of this age love to role-play the first step would be to take him to the bathroom as much as possible. He should be encouraged to sit on his potty, but do not remove his nappy just yet. Allowing him to watch you as you demonstrate and describe what you are doing, will go a long way to teaching your child in advance what will eventually be expected of him. The important thing at this stage is that he learns to sit still on the potty, while you explain what you are doing using clear simple language and actions. The following example illustrates the main points you want to get across to your child.

✿ *You say:* Mummy needs to go and do a pee pee
   Helpful action: take his hand and lead him to the bathroom

✿ *You say:* Mummy does pee pee in the loo
   Helpful action: show him the toilet, pointing where the pee pee goes

✿ *You say:* Mummy is pulling down her pants
Helpful action: demonstrate how you pull your pants down

✿ *You say:* Mummy is going to sit down on the loo and do pee
pee, and James can sit on his potty
Helpful action: applaud when he sits on his potty and praise
him by saying 'James is such a clever boy sitting so still on
his potty'

✿ *You say:* Mummy has finished pee pee and she's going to
pull up her pants
Helpful action: demonstrate how you pull your pants up

Jessica

aged 22 months

Elizabeth had followed the routines in *The Contented Little Baby Book* since her daughter Jessica was six days old. She had been a model baby sleeping through from 7pm to 7am with just a 10pm feed from eight weeks then right through from 7pm to 7am at four months. She also slept a good one and a half to two hours every lunchtime, until she was 22 months. Then one day when Elizabeth went in to wake Jessica up after her nap she was confronted with Jessica sitting completely naked in the cot covered from head to toe in poo. Elizabeth had such a shock at the unexpected sight that she let out a huge scream of horror. Jessica unaware that she was doing anything wrong, obviously got a fright by her mother's reaction and immediately burst into tears. Elizabeth picked the very messy Jessica up and tried to comfort her saying that Mummy would soon get all the smelly horrible poo cleaned up.

After she was cleaned up Jessica returned to being her normal happy cheerful self and the rest of the day followed as normal. However, that night when Elizabeth tried to settle Jessica in her cot she became hysterical and would not be put down. It took nearly two hours to get her off to sleep; she then woke up three times that night and had to be settled back to sleep each time. The following day at lunchtime Jessica totally refused to go in her cot, screaming each time her mother attempted to put her in it. That night followed the same pattern as the night before with Jessica screaming each time her mother took her near the cot. The following day Elizabeth took Jessica to the doctor convinced that she must have been coming down with an illness. Jessica was checked over thoroughly by the doctor and given a clean bill of health. The same pattern took place that night as on the previous two nights and it was the following day that Elizabeth rang me desperate for advice on what could be causing the sudden change in Jessica's sleeping.

On listening to Elizabeth's story I was convinced that the cause of the problem was linked to the day that Jessica woke up mid-way through her nap and took off her nappy. Elizabeth confirmed what I had suspected that Jessica had never ever seen her own poo. When her nappy was changed it was quickly folded up and put straight into the nappy bin, without any reference to its contents.

The first day that Jessica took off her nappy and discovered her poo she, like most children, was naturally curious about what she saw. However, I suspected it was her mother's reaction that left Jessica feeling very bad. And because the incident and her mother's shocked response happened when Jessica was in her cot, I believed it had created a bad sleep association.

While I am not suggesting that parents make a big deal when changing a toddler's nappy I always advise that they should occasionally let the toddler see the poo in the nappy. Saying something like, 'Lets get this poo all wrapped up before we put it in the bin'. Never, ever should it be called smelly or yucky. I have seen many toddlers come to have a real problem passing their poos because their parents have unintentionally made them feel bad about their natural bodily functions. For many children who have never seen a poo it can become a real problem when potty training if they think they are doing something nasty.

I advised that Elizabeth should continue to sit by the cot in the evening to settle Jessica, but that she should let Jessica see the contents of her nappy when she had done a poo. She should also take Jessica to the loo when she went herself and point out that Mummy also does poos.

Within a week Jessica was getting less and less fretful about going to bed, but still woke up briefly for reassurance once or twice a night. She was also very relaxed about her poos and was actually happy to do them in the potty. I told Elizabeth to continue reassuring Jessica for another week, then if we felt that she was still totally relaxed about doing her poos, we would do two or three nights of sleep training to get her back to sleeping 7pm to 7am.

Some child-care experts believe that the reason some toddlers and children have a fear of their poos and will hold back on doing them, is because they feel they are losing a part of themselves. They advise that it is better if the child doesn't see the poo being discarded. My own personal belief is that children of around one year of age should be made aware of what is in their nappy, and that parents adopting a relaxed attitude at such a young age is better than the child discovering his natural bodily functions the way Jessica did.

Understanding wet and dry

When you wash your hands encourage him to join in, washing and drying his own hands at the same time you are doing yours. Place a lot of emphasis on the words wet and dry, demonstrating how his hands become wet with water when washed, and then dry when wiped with the towel. Occasionally it is a good idea to wet the hand towel deliberately, allow him to feel the wet towel as you explain how much nicer it is to dry his hands on a clean dry towel. He should then be allowed to choose between the wet and the dry towel, for drying hands. This will help him to understand the difference and the importance between wet and dry.

When he shows signs of trying to copy you and participate in the above procedures, provided he is showing all the other signs of readiness for potty training you can start with Stage One on page 53.

Potty talk

Once the potty has been introduced it is important to decide which words you are going to describe the different parts of the body and their functions. If he is about to start nursery it might be a good idea to have a chat with the teacher to find out which words they use; 'pee and poo' seem to be the most popular ones, but 'wee' or 'number one' and 'number two' are also fairly common. However, it is best to check, as you do not wish your child to feel self-conscious on his first day at nursery if he announces he needs a wee wee when all the other children say pee. Once certain words have been decided it is important that everyone in the family sticks to using the same words during and after training.

When you begin training and your child is wearing pants it is also extremely important never to show signs of anger, disgust or disapproval when dealing with accidents in his pants.

I have often heard parents and carers saying something like 'Oh, you naughty boy what smelly wet knickers' or 'What a stinky poo'. Some young children are very sensitive about their bodily functions and take any disapproval of their pee or poos as a personal rejection. I have seen many young children develop real problems, particularly with having a bowel movement, simply because parents and carers have been very insensitive when dealing with accidents.

Case history

Leo

aged 30 months

Leo had been very enthusiastic about potty training and was completely dry by 25 months. Within a couple of weeks of being trained he was also happy to use the big loo for his wees. However, when it came to doing a poo he simply refused to use either the potty or the loo. No matter how desperate he was to open his bowels, he would hold on until he had his nappy on at his day-time nap or at bedtime. By the time I arrived to help care for Leo's newborn baby sister, opening his bowels had become a real problem. Sometimes he would go three or four days before eventually passing a very hard bowel motion in his nappy or pants. The discomfort of passing these hard bowel movements made Leo even more reluctant to sit on his potty or the loo.

While it is perfectly normal for some children to become dry long before they are clean, a problem like Leo's can quickly evolve if the refusal to poo in the potty or on the loo is handled badly. And within days of my arrival it was clear this was exactly what had happened to Leo. I observed that the nanny insisted that he sit on the loo several times a day and try to do a poo. She would make much talk about him being a big boy now, and how big boys don't do poos in their pants. He was constantly reminded of how clever his friends were for doing their poos in the potty, and how they would laugh at him for being such a baby. Each time he did a poo in his pants he was reprimanded and told how smelly and disgusting it was.

Although the nanny meant well, it was clear that her obsession with getting Leo to be clean was making him very anxious and causing him to hold back on his bowel movements. As we saw in Jessica's case, until children are potty trained, they may never actually have sight of their poo. Hence, when it is eventually shown to them and they are told how revolting it is (usually both at the same time) it can leave them with an association that is psychologically disturbing. Persistent retention of bowel movements can result in the child becoming very constipated, which in turn results in a great deal of pain when he does eventually go to the loo.

I suggested to the nanny and to Leo's parents that they should stop pressurising him to do a poo on the toilet or potty. During the following week no comment whatsoever was made when he filled his pants or nappy, since it was very important that words like 'smelly' and 'disgusting' were not used. I also advised them to keep increasing his intake of fruit and fluids until he was no longer constipated, and until he was having a bowel movement every day.

Once he was having a bowel movement each day they could then comment on how clever he was and how much easier it would be to do the soft poo on the toilet. It was essential that no other references were made regarding his bowel movements. Although it took nearly three weeks, Leo eventually went to the toilet of his own accord and passed a bowel movement.

His parents then introduced a column on his star chart and for every six stars in the potty column he was allowed a special treat. His parents continued to keep a very close watch on his diet, ensuring that it contained enough fruit, vegetables and fluid to help avoid constipation. Leo continues to use the big toilet and takes much pride in the size and colour of his poos!

Twins

Parents of twins often ask me if my advice will work when potty training two children at the same time. The answer is that the potty-training programme will work provided both children are showing signs of readiness at the same time. However, in my experience this is rarely the case, and to attempt to train them both together when one is showing all the signs and the other is not will only lead to disaster. It will only put the child who is not showing all the signs of readiness under emotional and perhaps physical pressure if potty training is forced before he is really ready.

If both children are showing all the signs of readiness I would give it a try but I try and enlist an extra pair of hands for the first few days to deal with all the wet pants and puddles.

If only one child is showing all the signs of readiness I would go ahead and train him, but I would try to arrange it so that the other child spends part of the day with someone else. This helps to avoid possible distractions and prevents the child who isn't ready being made to feel guilty.

In my experience, as long as no pressure is put on the second twin to use the potty, they will usually start to use it of their own accord in a very short space of time.

Guidelines when potty training twins

❀ Do not rush into potty training too quickly; wait until they are at least two years of age.

❀ It is often easier to potty train them separately, particularly if they have elder or younger siblings.

❀ Have a potty of the same design and colour for each child so that they do not fight over the same potty.

✿ If potty training both children be careful not to compare each one against the other. It should not become so competitive that one of the children begins to feel pressurised.

✿ Have more pants and face cloths than the recommended amount so that you are not under pressure if you get behind with the laundry.

Case history

Kate and Toby

aged 26 months

Susannah started on Stage One of potty training when the twins reached their first birthday. Both toddlers took to sitting on the potty well, first in the evening before their bath and then, after a couple of weeks, in the morning. They both showed all the signs that they were ready to be potty trained a month after starting Stage One and Susannah decided to take them out of nappies. The first day they both had lots of accidents, but Toby did manage to pee in the potty five times and Kate managed twice.

On the second day, Susannah decided to use a star chart as an incentive to encourage both toddlers to use the potty more. Toby who was the more placid of the twins happily co-operated and managed to get through the day with only three accidents. However, Kate, who had a much more independent and stubborn streak, started to rebel about using the potty and got very upset when her mother encouraged her to sit on it.

On the third day, Toby had only two accidents, but Kate began to get more and more hysterical about using the potty. Susannah rang me that night for advice; she was sure that Kate had shown all the right signs and couldn't understand why she had regressed so much. I assured her that this behaviour was fairly normal with twins and that she should continue to potty train Toby, but put Kate back in nappies until she herself asked her to go back into pants.

For the rest of the week Toby continued to do well using the potty with only the occasional accident. Every morning Susannah would put Kate into a nappy and tell her that she should let mummy know when she wanted to wear her big girl pants again.

By the middle of the second week Toby was completely dry most days, but Kate was still showing no signs of wanting to use the potty. Susannah was very worried that Kate was going to be difficult to train, but I reassured her that once Kate decided she was ready she would train just as quickly as Toby. The important thing was not to put any pressure on her and not even to attempt the preparation stage. It was a further month before Kate finally asked to put her big girl pants on, and within two days she was completely dry; Susannah didn't even have to use a star chart and rarely had to prompt her.

This case study is fairly typical of twins and as with all other stages of development, I always remind parents that each child is an individual and just because they are twins they should not expect them to advance at the same pace.

How to train – Stage One

If your child is happy to participate when you take him with you to the bathroom (see page 32) and shows all of the other signs of readiness for potty training on page 12, he should be encouraged to sit on his potty without his nappy while you prepare his bath. A time limit of five to ten minutes is long enough and if he manages to do anything in the potty remember to give him lots of praise. When praising your child it is important that he understands why you are pleased with him. For example, it is better to say how clever he is at sitting on his potty, or how clever he is at peeing in his potty. Try to avoid saying what a good boy he is, as he may start to think he is bad if he doesn't manage to make it to the potty.

Once he is happy to sit on the potty at bathtime, you should try sitting him on it after breakfast when he is changing out of his pyjamas and when you get him up from his nap. Again the nappy should be taken off and he should be encouraged to sit for a short spell on his potty. Don't worry if he doesn't manage to do anything, this is just practising.

Clean before dry

Many children are clean before they are dry, as it is easier for them to control their bowel than their bladders. If your child does a poo around the same time every day, it is worthwhile sitting him on the potty at that time, as well as the times mentioned on pages 53 and 54. It can be a bit hit and miss at this stage; sometimes a child will do a poo in the potty, other times he will do it the minute he puts his nappy on. If this happens do not make a fuss, simply change his nappy and tell him that the next time he needs a poo he should try to do it in his potty. The important thing is not to show disapproval or scold the child if he doesn't manage to poo in the potty every time. Encouragement and gentle reassurance will in the long term get better results. Occasionally, when a child is first introduced to the potty he will hold back on doing a poo, sometimes for two or three days and then will do it in his nappy. Try not to put pressure on him to do it in his potty, as this will only make matters worse. If he doesn't go for two or three days and he shows signs of constipation, try increasing the amount of fruit and vegetables he eats, and offer extra fluid. Once a child experiences passing hard poos it can lead to them becoming even more anxious about doing poos in the potty.

If he has been happy sitting on his potty at the previously mentioned times for at least a week, you can seriously consider putting him in pants and training him to use the potty during the day. However, as I should point out, the success of the potty training will depend not only on your child being ready, but also on you being ready. Even if your toddler is showing all of the correct signs and happily following Stage One, it would be inadvisable to go onto Stage Two of potty training unless you have the time to devote yourself to the task one hundred per cent.

Potty training is best avoided when:

❀ Either a new baby is due within a couple of months or a new baby has arrived within the last couple of months.

❀ You have just moved or about to move to a new house.

❀ Your child has recently recovered from an illness.

❀ There has been a change in child care circumstances.

❀ You or your husband are experiencing pressures at work.

❀ Either elder or younger siblings are going through sleeping difficulties or behavioural problems.

❀ Times such as Christmas or holidays when lots of social activities are planned.

Anastasia

aged 25 months

Anastasia was 21 months when her mother Sophie started to potty train her. She was a very bright little girl with a large vocabulary of words for her age. She had also started to show an interest in the potty and her mother was confident that she was ready to be potty trained. With a new baby due in a couple of months Sophie was keen to get Anastasia out of nappies before it arrived. She knew that the first few months after the baby was born would be very exhausting and she would not have time or the energy to potty train Anastasia. Within two weeks of starting the training Anastasia was both clean and dry during the day, with only the occasional accident of wet pants.

Anastasia was delighted when her baby brother James arrived and showed no signs of jealousy and she continued to use her potty or the toilet during the day with very little prompting from her mother.

Unfortunately her brother was a very difficult feeder, screaming during feeding and unsettled between most feeds. By the time James was five weeks Sophie was absolutely exhausted and finding it very difficult to cope with his frequent night waking and difficult behaviour during the day.

At his six-week check-up James was diagnosed with severe reflux and put on medication, which did help with his feeding. However he continued to be a very demanding baby and Sophie was finding it more and more difficult to cope with an energetic toddler and a demanding baby.

As the tension in the household grew Anastasia started to have the odd accident of wetting her pants, nearly always when James was being fed. Sophie had read that toddlers often had the occasional accident when a new baby arrived and tried to make light of the matter when these accidents happened. However, things came to a head when Sophie was having a particularly bad day with James and Anastasia not only wet herself three times in a row but also did a poo in her pants.

Sophie, by this time, was totally exhausted and at the end of her tether. She completely lost her temper and ended up smacking Anastasia. This of course made matters even worse and Anastasia, from then on, went on to have more and more accidents during the day. She also went from being a very out-going easy little girl to being fretful and withdrawn. She was 25 months when her mother rang me desperate for advice.

Although I normally advise parents never to put their children back in nappies once they are trained, there is always an exception to the rule, and this was certainly true in Anastasia's case. Because she had potty trained very young and was still only 25 months old, I advised Sophie to put her straight back into nappies for at least two months. This would allow Sophie time to get the baby sleeping through the night and hopefully the reflux condition would have improved making feeding time less demanding.

Sophie felt that it was a real admission of defeat to put Anastasia back in nappies, but I explained that it would be much more damaging to try and resolve the situation under such pressurised circumstances.

The younger a child is potty trained, the more likely they will be to regress in difficult circumstances. If a child is still under two years of age when a new baby arrives, I always feel it is better to delay potty training until a couple of months after the birth – even if the toddler is showing all the right signs. Then once the baby is sleeping through the night and is settled into a good day-time routine and the toddler shows no signs of resentment, potty training can be attempted.

Sophie actually waited until Anastasia was 28 months old; she then followed the preparation stage for three days, before going onto Stage Two of potty training. Anastasia was clean and dry within two days and has remained so ever since.

How to train – Stage Two

The majority of children are usually ready to go onto Stage Two somewhere between the first and second week of following Stage One. However, if your child is nearer three years old he may be ready to move on to Stage Two sooner. If your child shows all the signs of being ready to move onto Stage Two, but the time is not right for you or the rest of the family, continue with Stage One until the time is right. However, if you are confident that the time is right for you and that your child is showing all of the signs of being ready and is happily co-operating with the Stage One procedure, you should be able to successfully potty train him within one week.

It is very important to choose a week that is fairly free of activities, especially for the first couple of days. Explain to family and friends that you are potty training and you will be unavailable for telephone calls and visits during the daytime. If you have other children it is probably better to start at the weekend, when your husband can help out. To train your toddler quickly and successfully, it is very important not only that you are in a relaxed state of mind, but that any older or younger siblings are happy and in a good enough routine to allow one hundred per cent concentration and the extra time needed to achieve this.

Your toddler will need your constant attention and encouragement during the first couple of days; otherwise he will very quickly lose interest.

Where to train

The majority of advice that I have read advise parents that potty training should be done in the summer, so that the child can spend most of his day running around outside without his pants on. This is fine if your child just happens to be ready for potty training at that time of the year and the weather permits. I personally can't remember ever training a child this way as I have always taken the view that potty training is about exchanging nappies for pants, and that should be done from day one.

While I have often allowed a child to run around the first day or so without pants I don't see the point of allowing it to go on any longer than that. To me the whole concept of potty training is that the child learns the difference between wet and dry, and that is much easier to achieve when wearing pants. It also means that when accidents happen indoors most of the pee is soaked up into the pants and not the carpet.

Obviously there will be times when your child leaves a puddle on the floor, so during the first couple of days of training try to restrict training to just a couple of rooms. I suggest starting off the first morning of training in the kitchen so you can keep a close eye on the child while you are doing the chores. This also means that you can involve the child in things like washing up or baking and if accidents happen they are easily cleaned up.

When moving to another room with carpets I would put the potty on an old rug or doubled-up thick towel, because in my experience accidents nearly always happened near the potty when the child just didn't get there quite quick enough.

Hygiene

During the early stages of potty training you will need to wipe your toddler's bottom, and help him wash and dry his hands. By the time they get to three years most toddlers are becoming more independent and children insist on doing these things for themselves. It is important to help them practise how to wipe their bottoms properly (girls from front to back) and how to wash their hands thoroughly. The use of novelty soaps and cartoon illustrated hand cloths can help make hand washing and drying more fun. It is essential to teach your child the importance of proper hygiene from the very start of potty training.

The Seven Day
Programme

Day one

On the first day of training, once your toddler has had his breakfast, he should be put straight into his 'special big boy pants'. I generally leave trousers, shoes and socks off for the first couple of days as this makes it easier. If you have followed the steps listed in the preparation stage he will already have some idea of what is he is expected to do, so keep explanations and instructions as clear and as simple as possible. Explain simply that he is a big boy now and can wear pants like mummy and daddy, and that he can use his potty when he needs to do a pee-pee or poo. Also continue taking him with you to the bathroom and explaining what you are doing. Suggest he sits on his potty at the same time so you can both do a pee pee. Try to keep everything as relaxed and as positive as possible and never show any disapproval or disappointment when he has an accident. Try to keep the emphasis on how clever he is at sitting on his potty, and how grown up he is wearing big boy pants like daddy and mummy.

During the first couple of days he will need frequent reminders to sit on the potty. Therefore, it is better to try and contain the training to one room. If you have to move between two rooms make sure that you are prepared with a selection of books already in each room. Should you need to go to the other room for even a few minutes, it is important that you take the toddler and the potty. He should be encouraged to sit on the potty every fifteen minutes, ideally for a period of five to ten minutes each time. If necessary sit next to him on the floor and read the books together. Some children are happy to sit longer, and others get bored very quickly. If your child is one of the latter encourage him to look at a book or sing along to his cassette tape. Once he has successfully used the potty several times, the length of time between reminders can be gradually extended.

The length of time it takes for a child to use the potty several times successfully varies from child to child. Some of the children I have trained are peeing regularly in the potty within a couple of hours; with others it can take several hours, and there have been a few where it has been well into the second day before any reasonable results are got. Do not despair if your child wets his pants several times before he manages to do it in the potty. Once he does manage to pee in it a couple of times in a row, he will be so proud of himself that he will be very keen to keep showing you his new skill.

Dealing with accidents

Do not be disappointed if your child has lots of accidents the first day, this does not mean that he is not ready to be potty trained. Some of the toddlers I have trained have gone through all their pants within a few hours.

The important thing is not to make a big fuss or show displeasure when he does have an accident. Change his pants and continue to be enthusiastic about his big boy pants and how clever he is at sitting on his potty. When he is successful at using the potty, tell him how clever he is at peeing in the potty and how happy and proud your partner will be. Lots of praise, hugs and applause along with the use of a star chart is the most effective way of encouraging him to continue using the potty. All children respond better to encouragement and praise rather then criticism. The star chart will also be a visible reminder of how clever his is at using the potty.

Remember to have a small bucket with warm water, disinfectant and a cloth at hand (but out of reach of your child) to quickly clean up any messes. At this stage do not make any comment when cleaning up the mess, as you do not want to draw your child's attention to his failure to make it to the potty. A small bucket filled with a cold-water soap powder solution to drop wet or soiled pants into is also useful. To get rid of any excess poo on his pants, using gloves hold them over the loo and flush a couple of times.

I have also found it very useful to keep a second chart for myself detailing the progress of potty training. It is a great help to see a pattern emerging of how often he needs to pee and whether successful use of the potty was self motivated or not.

You can draw a simple chart like the one opposite; simply record each time he pees by ticking the appropriate column. In the potty column use one tick when he urinates in the potty after being instructed by you, and two ticks when he urinates in the potty of his own accord.

POTTY PROGRESS CHART

Time	Potty	Accident	Comments

By the end of the first day there should be more ticks in the potty column than in the accident column. If your child is under 28 months and has no ticks in the potty column it is clear that for whatever reason he is not yet ready and it would be better to go back to the preparation stage for a further week or two.

In my experience, a child who has shown all the signs of readiness and has followed all the preparation instructions laid out in Stage One, will probably have at least two or three ticks in the potty column.

However, if your child is nearer three years of age it is probably worth trying for a second day even if he hasn't managed to do anything in the potty.

At the end of the first day, regardless of how successful he was at using his potty, it is important to tell your child how proud you are of him for being so clever at using his potty. No reference should be made to any accidents that have occurred during the day. Also it helps to reinforce the idea of wearing pants if you get

  Potty Training in One Week

him to choose the ones he will wear the following day.

To help avoid boredom setting in during the second day of training try to arrange for one of his friends to come round for a short play date. This can be used as a further encouragement to your child, for example, 'Tommy will be so excited to see you in your big boy pants when he visits tomorrow'.

Helpful guidelines for surviving Day one

✿ The point to remember on Day one is that it is not important how many times your child pees in the potty. The most important thing is that he is happy to sit on it for short spells at regular intervals throughout the day.

✿ Do not get despondent if your child has lots of accidents. As long as he has shown all the signs of readiness and happily followed Stage One for a short period a couple of pees in the potty by the end of the first day is fine.

✿ When he does manage to do a pee on the potty, no matter how small, give lots of praise smiles and cuddles. Remember also to praise him when he sits on the potty, not just when he pees in it.

✿ When explaining to your child what is expected of him it is important that you get down to his level so that you have eye to eye contact when talking. Never shout instructions across the room and assume that he has taken in what you have said.

✿ When he has an accident it is very important to stay calm and make light of it. For example, try not to show your anger if he misses the potty by a couple of inches. Say something like, 'Never mind, you nearly made it to the potty, let's go and put some nice clean dry pants on'.

✿ Try to have a variety of different activities planned throughout the day. Drawing, jigsaws, collages and anything that can be done at the kitchen table is a good idea. Try to save reading stories and watching videos for times when he appears not to be so interested in using a potty. If he has gone a couple of hours without doing a pee, encourage him to sit on his potty and read him a story or sit with him and watch a video for a short spell.

✿ Avoid using the phone during the first day and keep any visits from unexpected callers as brief as possible. It is important to devote yourself one hundred per cent to observing, encouraging and helping your child master potty training.

Day two

By the second day of training your chart (see page 75) should begin to show a pattern of more regular intervals between the times your child needs to pass urine. This pattern will serve as a guide as to how often you need to remind him, and how often he is using the potty of his own accord. Obviously the aim is that he needs less and less reminders from you, and there are fewer accidents. For this to happen it is important that the potty is still kept within full view and within easy reach.

As the day progresses you should gradually go from reminding him to sit on the potty, to asking him if he needs to use the potty. It is important for his mental and physical awareness that you start to allow him some of the responsibility of deciding when he needs to use the potty, even if it means occasional accidents. Accidents will be more likely to happen if your child is playing and forgets or gets excited.

If you can see a particular pattern occurring on your chart, then you should be able to use it to tell when to go from suggesting that he sits on his potty to reminding him where it is if he needs to use it.

Remember to invite a friend for your child to prevent him from getting bored. It is even better if his friend is potty trained; as he will be more than likely keen to show off his potty and big boy pants.

Helpful guidelines for surviving Day two

✿ Do not get despondent if he is still having quite a few
   accidents. As long as he is still eager to use the potty and
   has managed a couple of pees in the potty during the
   second day you can be sure you are on the right track. A
   few of the children I have trained seem to have endless
   accidents the first couple of days, then suddenly it all falls
   into place by the third day.

✿ Try to arrange activities that are not too boisterous and could lead your child to becoming very over-excited and forgetting about the potty altogether.

✿ If playing out of doors it is important to take the potty out with you and place it in a very prominent place. It often helps if you let your child decide where he would like it to be put.

✿ By the end of the second day you should begin to feel that you are getting somewhere with potty training and that your child is grasping what is expected of him.

Potty Training in One Week

Day three

By the third day a definite pattern should have emerged as to how often he needs to use the potty. The progress chart should be of help when planning the best time for your first outing. Ideally it should be a short visit to one of his friends who lives close by. Before leaving the house your toddler should be encouraged to use the potty so as to avoid any accidents on the journey. Do not be tempted to put him back into a nappy or disposable pull-up trainer pants on outings, as this will only give confusing signals and is one of the main reasons why potty training can take so long.

Consistency is of the utmost importance if you want to potty train quickly and successfully. Dress your toddler in pants at all times during the day – nappies are for sleep times only. While there may be a few accidents during the first few days, these mishaps will actually help your child to become more aware of his need to pee, and the difference between wet and dry. It is best not to make a fuss or scold your toddler if he has an accident, simply remind him what the potty is for.

In the early days it is advisable to take a couple of spare changes of clothes and pants on outings and a plastic bag to put them in if they get wet. And always remember his special cushion (see page 27) when travelling in the car or using the buggy. Until your toddler gets used to using the loo you will also need to take his potty. Although I have never personally used one, there are special portable potties now available for travelling.

Guidelines that will help during Day three:

❀ The important thing when going on an outing is not to be tempted to put him back into nappies or trainer pants. This will only confuse your child and in my experience flitting back and forth from pants to nappies is one of the main reasons why potty training can take so long for many parents.

✿ Accept that there may be an accident when you are out and go well equipped with two sets of changes of outer clothes and pants, a plastic bag to put any wet clothes in as well as his special cushion.

✿ Before you leave the house take your child and his potty with you to the bathroom, explain that 'Mummy is going to sit on the loo and do a pee, and that he should sit on his potty as well', encourage him to sit for five to ten minutes by reading him a story. Some parents maintain that running the cold tap while sitting the child on the potty often encourages them to do a pee. It will do no harm to try this if nothing has happened within five minutes. Once ten minutes have elapsed I would not insist that he sits any longer. I would prepare for the outing, which should ideally only be a ten-minute journey away, and trust to luck that you get there without any accidents.

✿ Until your child is used to and confident about using the big loo, you will need to take his potty with you. There are travel potties available, but unless you plan to do lots of longer journeys it is probably not worth buying one. Hopefully your child will be used to using the big loo regularly within a couple of weeks of being trained.

Case history

Libby

aged 29 months

Melissa first started potty training her daughter Libby when she was only about 22 months of age. She showed all the right signs of being ready for potty training and would happily sit on her potty, first thing in the morning, after lunch and before her bath. More often than not she would do something in the potty, so Melissa started to leave her nappy off for short spells at other times of the day.

Although she rarely used her potty at these times she never had any accidents. When Libby reached two years of age Melissa enrolled her in an organised playgroup three mornings a week in order to prepare her for going to nursery full time when she returned to work. Melissa decided to put Libby into pants at this stage as she was showing such good signs of controlling her bladder.

Libby really enjoyed the playgroup but was prone to getting very excited when playing and started occasionally to wet her pants. Changing her pants in the midst of all the excitement often led to tantrums and on the advice of several other mothers Melissa began to put Libby into pull-up nappies for playgroup.

Things reverted back to normal and Libby happily used her potty three times a day and went without nappies for short spells in the afternoon when at home.

However, a problem arose about three weeks before Libby was about to start nursery. Melissa decided to put Libby into pants all the time during the day on the days she didn't go to playgroup, to prepare her for the nursery, which had a policy that all children must be potty trained.

Because Libby had always been so good about going on her

potty at regular times, Melissa was shocked when Libby then started to have tantrums about going on the potty. The tantrums were soon followed by lots of wet pants. Because this behaviour was only on the days Libby was at home Melissa thought that perhaps Libby wasn't really ready after all to be totally potty trained. Two weeks prior to Libby starting full-time nursery Melissa rang me desperate for advice.

From the details Melissa gave me Libby certainly appeared to have given all the correct signals that she was ready for potty training. I believed the problems Melissa was experiencing were caused by the fact that she had confused Libby by putting her back into nappies for part of the day.

This is one of the most common reasons why potty training can take so long for many parents and why other problems can occur.

I advised Melissa to spend three days back on the preparation stage, then go straight into Stage Two of actual training, and under no circumstances should she put Libby back in nappies, especially on the day she went to playgroup. It is better to deal with a number of accidents for a week or so than spend months going back and forth between nappies and pants. The first three days Libby only managed to pee in her potty a couple of times, but by the fourth day things were getting better. Within a week Libby was totally dry. I believe that this could have happened from the very onset of potty training if Melissa had not confused Libby by switching back and forth from nappies to pants.

Days four to seven

By the fourth day the majority of toddlers are regularly using their potty without prompting, with just the occasional accident occurring. Over the next few days the potty should gradually be moved nearer and nearer to the bathroom. Once your toddler shows signs that he can control his bladder long enough to get to the bathroom, it should remain there permanently. If a couple of hours have gone by without him using the potty, and he seems particularly engrossed in something, it would be advisable to remind him where the potty is. But try not to nag him about it; it is much better to allow him to take the lead at this stage and to have the odd accident, than end up in a situation where he becomes dependent on you reminding him, or worse, rebels totally against potty training because he feels under constant pressure.

By the end of the first week it is also a good idea to introduce your child to using the big loo. In my experience the sooner the child is encouraged to use the big loo, the less likely he is to become frightened of it. You could ask either his grandparents or one of his favourite aunts to send him a special loo seat as a reward for being such a clever boy at wearing pants. By making the loo seat appear as a reward he will be much more accepting of it. However, it is important to be very gentle when putting him on it and reassure him that you will kneel down and stay right beside him until he has finished. He may still wish to use his potty some of the time, but do try to get him to use both the potty and the big loo by the end of the first week.

The majority of toddlers are dry most of the time by the end of the first week, with only the occasional accident.

Guidelines to help you through Days four to seven

❀ To ensure continued success it is important that you never put your toddler back in nappies apart from sleep times. It only confuses the toddler and is one of the main reasons potty training can become a problem and take many months to crack.

❀ By the end of the first week you should aim towards getting your child used to going to the bathroom when he needs to do a pee or a poo. Gradually move the potty nearer and nearer to the bathroom, so that it eventually ends up in the bathroom permanently.

❀ Once you have established that the bathroom is where he now does his pee and poo, you can now encourage him to use the big loo. Always use one of the specially designed seats that fit over the loo, get down to his level and hold him on the loo under his arms until he becomes more confident about holding onto the handles of the child seat. He may also feel more confident if you have a little step for him to rest his feet on.

✿ His star chart and stickers can be used as an incentive to use the big loo. Buy some extra big stars to put on the chart for when he uses the big loo. If he has more than three big stars on his chart by teatime he could be given a treat of an ice-cream or his favourite biscuit after his tea.

✿ Finally, it is important to remember that most children under three years will continue to have an occasional accident, particularly if they are over-excited during play or over-tired. While it is important not to get angry or punish them, I would insist that they help clear up any mess, so that they learn that peeing or pooing anywhere other than the potty or loo does have its consequences.

Case study

Samuel

aged 3 years

Samuel was not potty trained until he was 33 months. Because he was older and showed all the right signs of being ready Helen, his mother, spent only three days on the preparation stage before going onto Stage Two of actual potty training. Within a couple of days Samuel was both clean and dry during the day and at his own request abandoned the nappy during his short nap in the middle of the day.

Things went very well for the first couple of months with virtually no accidents. Then about a month before his third birthday he started to have one or two accidents most days, things got increasingly worse and by the time he reached his third birthday he was having several accidents a day.

Helen could think of no obvious reason for this backtrack and rang me for advice. After a 20-minute chat it was obvious that while Helen thought she had followed the potty training programme to the letter, she had missed one important piece of advice. This was that once Samuel was going to the potty at regular intervals, she did not allow him any responsibility to decide for himself when he needed to use the potty. Although Samuel's chart showed that he was managing to go between two to two and a half hours between using the potty, Helen had continued to remind him every 45 minutes or so to sit on it.

I advised Helen that she should ask Samuel the following morning where he would like to place his potty, and tell him that she was not going to remind him when to use it as he is a big boy now and can decide for himself when he needed to go. If and when he had an accident, she would not make a fuss or get angry, but gently remind that he must remember to make time to get to the potty the next time he needed a pee. She should also make him change his own pants and put the dirty ones in the soak bucket. On the occasions he did make it to the potty she should give him lots of praise, plus a smartie. Within two days Samuel was back to being completely dry and clean during the day and using the big loo. Within a week Helen had weaned him off the smartie for each time he used the big loo and offered him instead an ice-cream or a treat after tea.

From the many calls I have received from parents looking for advice, it has become clear that not allowing the child, particularly older children, to take some of the responsibility for deciding if they need to use the potty or loo, is a common cause of regression.

Sleep times

I would continue to put a toddler in nappies during his daytime sleep until his nappy has been consistently dry on waking for at least two weeks. After that I would feel confident it was safe to abandon it. For the night-time sleep, I would continue with nappies for several months. In my experience very few children are capable of going through the night before the age of three years, and with boys it may even be later.

I have found that parents who push night-time training before this age often end up with other problems. One major problem is that if the nappy is abandoned too early it is usually necessary either to install a night-light or leave the door slightly ajar so that the child can see his way to the potty or loo. With toddlers under three years the temptation to start running around in the middle of the night is often too hard to resist, especially if they know mummy is attending to a younger sibling. With a child over three years who is consistently dry and clean, I would explain that he no longer needs to wear a nappy at night and make sure that he goes on the potty just before he gets into bed so that he shouldn't need to wee during the night. This can also be helped by making sure that the last drink is given at least an hour before bedtime.

Beatrice

aged 27 months

Beatrice was just over two years old when her mother started potty training her and she was both clean and dry by the end of the first week. During the weeks that followed she rarely had any accidents and her nappy was dry most mornings. When she reached 26 months her mother was confident that she was ready to abandon the night-time nappy. Beatrice continued to stay dry both during the day and at night for a further two weeks. Then suddenly one morning at around 5am, Beatrice's parents were woken up by hysterical screaming. Beatrice, who had always slept soundly from 7pm to 7am, was inconsolable. It was clear that she wasn't ill, but her parents could not fathom what had caused the waking. It was not until twenty minutes later, when she had eventually calmed down, that she asked for her potty. At this stage her parents did not see the connection of her wanting to use the potty with the waking, as she had been dry at night for so many weeks.

However, the next night the same thing happened again and they then decided to put the potty in her room. They placed it next to a small night-light and explained to her that if she woke in the night and needed to wee, her potty was right beside her.

That night Beatrice did not settle well at 7pm. She kept getting out of bed, running around the room opening drawers and cupboards and shouting for her parents. After many return visits by her parents to Beatrice's room and several sittings on the potty, she eventually settled to sleep at 9pm.

She continued to be difficult to settle at night and after a couple of weeks her parents started to experience problems settling her for the daytime nap. The late bedtime and shorter lunchtime nap resulted in her becoming overtired, irritable and very fretful during the day. Realising that they now had a serious sleep problem on their hands, they contacted me for help.

I suggested that they try the method used for a late bedtime problem (see *From Contented Baby to Confident Child*, page 103), bringing Beatrice's bedtime forward to avoid her becoming overtired, along with the advice for dealing with a toddler who keeps getting out of bed (*From Contented Baby to Confident Child*, page 108).

After two weeks Beatrice was settling well at night, at naptime, and also after using her potty in the night. I believe that Beatrice's problem was definitely caused by her parents taking her out of night-time nappies too early, which meant installing a potty and a night-light in her room. Very few children under three years of age have enough bladder control to sleep a 12-hour night.

In my experience, toddlers under three years of age who are sleeping in a bed, and who need to have a night-light are much more likely to wake in the night and be difficult to settle back to sleep. Hence my advice that parents of toddlers under three years who wish to avoid sleep problems, should think seriously before abandoning the sleep bag and cot which help to restrict a toddler who attempts to take his nappy off.

Problems

Problem
Solving

The stubborn child

Occasionally I have encountered a child who refuses to go on the potty and if he is under two and a half years I would not force the issue. However, with a child nearer three years of age who refuses to sit on the potty I would probably resort to bribery. I know the majority of experts would frown upon this advice, but sometimes, especially with a very stubborn child, it is the only way.

While a child over three years may not show all the signs necessary for potty training, he is usually capable of being trained. I would skip the preparation stage and go straight into potty training and use a star chart. I would explain that every time he does a pee in the potty he will get a star – and for every star he would get a treat. The treat can be a raisin or a very small sweet like a smartie. Believe me it does work, provided of course the child receives no other treats throughout the day. Within two

Potty Training in One Week

days I find the child is regularly asking for the potty – then the star, followed by the treat. Once I see a regular pattern emerge I explain to the child 'I have run out of the treats'.

I then suggest that the next three pees in the potty would deserve a trip to the shop for a special ice-cream. By using delaying tactics of a bigger treat for more pees in the potty, I eventually arrive at a stage where the child uses the potty throughout the day, and ends up with only one treat in the evening.

Guidelines for dealing with a stubborn child

❀ Using sweets, biscuits or ice-cream as a reward will only work if your child only gets these things when he has had a star for peeing or doing a poo in his potty. If your child receives these treats as a matter of course every day, then there will be no incentive for him. Restrict treats to those times that he has done something to achieve them.

- ❀ Once a pattern has emerged it is important to start delaying the treat tactics so that your child is not in control of the bargaining power.

- ❀ With a stubborn child over three years of age who refuses to use the potty, it is worthwhile looking at how he deals with taking instructions in the other areas in his life. If he is stubborn about a variety of different tasks, thought must be put into why this is happening. Often it occurs because parents are in disagreement about rules and boundaries. With no set rules and boundaries the child very quickly realises that by being stubborn he can end up controlling virtually every area of his life.

- ❀ If you come to the conclusion that nearly all your reasonable requests are being met with refusal or stubbornness it would be worthwhile seeking professional help or attending one of the many parenting workshops that are now available, before you even attempt potty training.

Bed-wetting

It is fairly common for young children to have an occasional accident at night. However, it can be a real problem if the bed-wetting becomes a regular occurrence. The broken nights' sleep changing wet sheets can be exhausting for parents and lead to the child feeling anxious and guilty. If your child has been dry for many weeks and suddenly starts wetting the bed, a visit to the doctor should be considered to rule out the possibility of a urinary infection. Many experts suggest that a relapse may be also caused by emotional problems; in my experience this is rarely the case. The majority of the parents I have worked with believe that excessive amounts of fluid prior to bedtime can be a major cause of a bed-wetting; therefore they allow no drinks after 6pm.

With a child under four years who has only been dry for a few weeks, and then starts to wet the bed regularly, it is probably because he isn't quite ready to go all night. It may be preferable to put him back in night-time nappies for a short while, thus avoiding bed-wetting becoming an issue.

If your child is over four years of age and despite restricting fluids you are still getting a wet bed every morning, it may be worthwhile lifting him and putting him on the potty at your bedtime. If this doesn't seem to work I would advise seeking professional help from your GP to try and get to the root of the problem.

Lifting at 10pm

Years ago child care experts advised parents to lift their baby at 10pm, and put him on the potty to pass urine. These experts believed that the age at which a child gained bladder control at night depended largely on the mother's skill in training him in infancy.

The child care manuals written in the 1930s and 1940s stressed that lifting should be a habit that is formed in infancy. Mothers were advised that regularity of lifting the child every night until he was four years old was key to teaching him how to stay dry throughout the night. If their laziness prevented them from doing this, they would create a habit difficult to cure. A child who got used to waking up with a wet nappy would quickly begin to believe that it was normal.

While many parents do still lift their children at their bedtime, the majority of child care experts today are against this practice. They believe this approach only conditions the child to pass urine at certain times. I would tend to agree with this, and would only consider lifting a child if he was over four years of age and, despite monitoring fluids in the evening, the bed was wet every morning.

A nanny friend and myself successfully used the lifting approach as a last resort when working in the Middle East with a family of serious bed-wetters. The six children aged between four and fourteen years were taken to the loo very sleepily at different times in the late evening. Occasionally one or the other would wake up wet, but much to the relief of the laundry staff, most mornings the beds were dry.

If you decide to try this approach, it is important that the child is kept sleepy and not stimulated. The lights should be kept very dim, and talking, if any, kept to a minimum. Children under three years could be put on the potty, instead of being taken to the bathroom. Some experts claim that varying the time of lifting will help reduce the possibility of conditioning the child's need to pee at the same time every night.

If you find that lifting your child is working, it is worthwhile using a star chart. On the mornings when the bed is dry he gets a star, three stars and he gets a special treat – perhaps an ice-cream.

If the bed-wetting improves, I would tell your child that he is a big boy now and doesn't need lifting any more in the night. Suggest to him that if he does wake in the night and needs a pee to call for you to come and help him. Although it will mean you getting up in the night for a short while, I usually find that the child will, as his confidence increases, be persuaded to use the potty by himself.

Again, I have found that if used properly a star chart can be very effective during these various stages.

Guidelines on lifting at night-time

❀ If your child is over four years of age and wetting the bed almost every night despite monitoring fluids, it would be advisable to discuss things with your GP to rule out any medical causes. If he rules out a medical reason it may be worthwhile lifting your child at night to see if this resolves the problem.

❀ Vary the time you lift your child so that he does not become conditioned to peeing at the same time every night.

❀ If the bed-wetting improves try introducing a start chart and reward if he gets up in the night to pee in his pot, or if his bed is dry in the morning. Occasionally I have found this to work if the cause of the problem is simply because the child is a bit lazy at getting out of bed in the middle of the night. However, a star chart would not work if there were other more psychological, emotional or medical reasons.

Regression

All toddlers and children will continue to have the occasional accident once they are potty trained. The important thing is to stay calm and consistent, and not be tempted to put him back into nappies if you have a bad couple of days. Occasionally a toddler or child who has been dry for many months may completely regress. This often happens around the time of a new brother or sister, starting playgroup or a similar emotional upheaval. If your child suddenly regresses and appears to be more withdrawn or is more demanding and displaying unusual aggressive behaviour, the regression is probably psychological. If his behaviour is normal it may be worth a visit to the doctor to rule out possibility of a urine infection.

Whatever has caused the regression I would advise only going back to nappies as a last resort. Although it may mean many wet pants for a short spell, being patient, consistent and encouraging will eventually get your child back on track. It is also worthwhile doing a progress chart (see page 75) for a couple of days to establish how often the accidents are happening. A pattern usually emerges as to how often he is having an accident, and this will enable you to remind him to use the potty at these regular intervals. If he is reluctant to use the potty, take him with you when you need to go to the loo yourself. Making a game of using the loo at the same time will often encourage him to go on the potty, while you are using the loo. Obviously this plan is more likely to be successful if done at roughly the times you think he may need to pee.

Re-introducing a line on his star chart for successful use of the potty can also be an incentive, particularly if used in conjunction with a sweet or a treat.

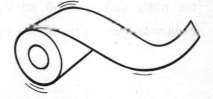

Potty Training Questions and Answers

Q My son is 16 months and showing no awareness when he does a wee or a poo, but my mother keeps nagging me to start training. Do you think he is ready?

A Very few children have the muscle control required for potty training before the age of 18 months and the majority are not ready until nearer two years of age. However, if the following statements are true for your child it may mean he is ready:

❀ His nappy should sometimes be dry when you get him up from his longest nap, or dry a couple of hours since his last nappy change.

❀ He understands and is capable of following simple instructions such as bring me your shoes, or sit here until Mummy gets your jacket.

Potty Training in One Week

✿ He should be content to sit by himself and play with his toys or look at a simple book for at least 10 minutes.

✿ He should be capable of taking off his socks and shoes, and attempting to pull down his shorts or trousers.

Q My 18 month-old toddler points to her nappy when she does a poo, but shows none of the other signs. Should I attempt to potty train her?

A It is unwise to start potty training until the child is clearly showing nearly all the signs. But you can begin to prepare her for potty training by doing the following:

❀ Buy a potty and leave it in the bathroom, explaining what it is for and encouraging her to sit on it for a few minutes before she gets in the bath. Under no circumstances force the issue at this stage, allow her to take the lead.

❀ Take her to the bathroom when you go and explain what you are doing. But do not ask her if she wants to use her potty. Let her take the lead, she will very quickly start to copy you and sit on her potty.

✿ Start encouraging her to pull down and pull up her shorts by herself. Give lots of praise when she manages to do it by herself.

✿ When she is playing with slightly older children, ask them if they mind her watching how clever they are at doing a wee on the potty or loo. Obviously if the other children are not keen to perform, do not force the issue.

✿ At bathtime and when she washes her hands, put lots of emphasis on the difference between the words wet and dry. Face cloths are a great way to demonstrate this. After a while ask her to show you the wet one, then the dry one.

Q We are going on holiday soon and my husband reckons that it would be a good time to begin training our toddler, as he could assist by helping with our young baby. What do you advise?

A I would not advise potty training on holiday. It would be unfair to expect the child to give potty training the concentration it requires, when he is excited about being on holiday.

During the first couple of days of potty training it is much better if there are as few people around as possible, thus avoiding too many distractions.

If you have a young baby try to start training at the weekend so your husband can take care of the baby, allowing you to concentrate on the training. Make sure your husband has done a trial run of caring for the baby before you actually start the potty training. The less interruptions when you are training the better.

Q Should I reward my child with a sweet or a treat when he is successful at using the potty.

A It is better if you can avoid this type of bribery. A child under two years will normally be happy with a star chart and lots of encouragement and praise.

Occasionally, if I am training an older child with a very stubborn streak, I do compromise. I explain that once he has three stars on his chart he will get a small treat. Once he is using the potty regularly, I tell him that when he has six stars on the chart he will get an ice-cream. This approach helps minimise the risk of the child only using the potty if he gets a reward.

Q What should I dress my child in during the potty training period?

A During the first two to three days when in the house it will be easier if you dress him in a very short t-shirt that does not need to be pulled up when he sits on the potty. He should also wear pants that are big enough to be easily pulled up and down.

When you have to take him out it is important that he continues to wear pants. Never go back to nappies once you've started, even if there are accidents. It's too confusing for the child and the main reason why potty training often fails.

Do not be tempted to use pull-up nappies. It will also confuse your child. Parents who use these on outings to avoid accidents take much longer to potty train their child, as the absorbency of the pull-ups decreases the child's awareness of being wet and dry.

Ensure that the outer garments are as simple as possible. Avoid lots of buttons, poppers or braces. Tracksuit bottoms or shorts and a loose short top are ideal.

Q My daughter aged two years and eight months has been dry for over six months, but she refuses to poo in her potty or the toilet. She always waits until she has her nappy on and then does it.

A This is a very common problem. In my experience it is more common amongst children who have irregular or hard bowel movements. It is worthwhile giving her more fruit to eat especially at breakfast time, and increasing the amounts of fluids she has. This often helps regulate the child's bowel movements. Once a regular time is established, line her potty with a nappy and encourage her to sit on it at that time. As a special treat let her watch her favourite video. Once she is regularly having a bowel movement, pretend to run out of nappies. With the help of a new book or video, she may be persuaded to use the potty without the nappy in it.

If this fails it is best not to force the issue, just accept she is going to poo in her nappy. The problem usually sorts itself out once the child is out of nappies altogether. However I would not advise taking her out of nappies at sleep times too quickly, just to solve this problem. All too often I have seen children completely back track with potty training because of pressure from parents or carers.

It is important never to attempt to break this habit by showing disgust at the dirty nappy, or scolding her. This sort of disapproval could lead to her becoming very worried and anxious, and withholding the poo altogether.

Q When should I start getting my daughter to use the toilet instead of the potty?

A Once she has developed enough bladder control to reach her potty in the bathroom, she should be encouraged to use the big toilet. It is best to insert a specially designed child's toilet seat that fits securely inside the big seat. The ones that are padded appear to be more popular with young children and some come with handles for them to hold on to, which is even better.

The toilet can seem very big and frightening to a toddler. To avoid long-term problems with using the toilet it is important that you not only hold her around her waist, but that you kneel down so you are face to face. Proper eye contact with her will help reassure her that nothing awful is going to happen.

Once you feel your toddler is confident about sitting on the big toilet, hold her with only one hand. As her confidence increases continue to get down to her level so she doesn't feel intimidated or alone, but encourage her to sit, while supporting herself. These few very simple measures will ensure that she quickly builds up her confidence to sit on the seat unaided.

Q My son is two and half years and has been clean and dry for nearly three months, but still sits when he needs to wee. At what age will he be capable of standing up and peeing?

A Many boys are nearer three years of age before they start to wee standing up. This is usually around the same time they start nursery and see how other boys are doing it. All children love to copy, so encourage him to go to the loo with daddy or other boys as much as possible.

If he is still not quite tall enough to aim into the loo easily, he may need to stand on a small step. He may need to be held under the arms until he learns to balance confidently by himself.

He may also need assistance in the early days in learning how high to hold his willy up, so he aims into the loo. When he is finished teach him to shake his willy over the loo, to avoid drips on the carpet.

If he is unsure or reluctant about standing up and peeing into the loo try getting him to pee into a disposable plastic cup over the loo. This trick seems to have worked with many of my little boys who have been hesitant about using the loo.

Q Once he is successfully potty trained how long do I wait before taking him out of nappies at sleep times?

A Continue to use nappies at the lunchtime nap. If he is consistently dry when he gets up for at least two weeks, you could then abandon the nappies.

For the night-time sleep I usually wait until the child is at least three years of age. If on waking his nappy is dry or only slightly damp for several weeks, you could then abandon the night-time nappy.

If you find he then starts to wake up in the night needing his potty, at this age he should be capable of getting out of bed and using the potty by himself. Obviously you would have to then install a small very dim night-light in his room.

I have found that installing a night-light with very young children can often lead to disturbed sleep and more night waking, so try and avoid this until he is nearer three years.

Q Is it advisable to use a waterproof sheet once he is out of night-time nappies?

A There are special water-proof pads that can go across the middle of the bed which can help when accidents occur.

If your child is one of the few who does not like the feel of these pads, use a water-proof sheet on top of the mattress, then the fitted sheet, then a further pad and finally a further fitted sheet. This way if your child does have an accident in the night, you can simply whip away the first two layers, and avoid having to remake the bed completely.

Finally remember that your child should not have excessive drinks before bedtime. A cup of milk should be given no later than 6pm and if still thirsty at bedtime offer a small amount of water.

Q My three-year-old son manages to stay dry most nights and we are thinking of taking him out of night nappies. My mother has suggested we should lift him at our bedtime and put him on the potty to avoid a wet bed.

A Many parents believe that lifting their child to wee at their bedtime encourages night training. Some experts believe that this practise only conditions the child to pass urine at certain times and actually delays the child learning night-time bladder control.

In my experience I have found it better to accept an occasional wet bed. The child then learns to control his bladder naturally and get up to use the potty when he needs to. However, if a child were over four years of age and regularly wetting the bed I would consider lifting him.

Before abandoning the night nappy, check the amount he is drinking at bedtime. If it is a huge amount, gradually cut back. Explain to him that he must have his big drink before 6pm, as he will only be allowed a small drink of water at bedtime.

Once you are happy that he is not drinking an excessive amount at bedtime, explain he is a big boy now and no longer needs to wear a nappy at bedtime. Ensure that he goes on the potty just before he gets into bed.

If you find you are getting the occasional accident, install a night-light and leave a potty in his room. Explain that he should use the potty in the night when he needs to do a wee.

Once he is older his door can be left slightly open so he can make his way to the bathroom.

Q My mother says that my two sisters and I were potty trained by the time we were eighteen months old and that I should start putting my son who is nearly 13 months old on the potty after every feed. I obviously believe my mother when she says that we were all trained so early, but I have read that beginning potty training too early can be psychologically damaging.

A Do not give in to pressure from well-meaning relatives and friends because attempting to potty train your child before she is physically and emotionally ready could lead to her feeling pressurised and cause her to rebel and resent using the potty. I have come across many children who have developed serious long-term problems with constipation and anxiety about doing a pee because their parents introduced the pot too early. Wait until your child is showing all the signs listed on page 12 before introducing her to the potty.

Children under 18 months rarely have developed the muscle control required for potty training. While I do not dispute that your mother managed to get you all out of nappies and trained by 18 months, it probably took her nearly six months of training instead of a week of training when done at the right moment.

If you wish to avoid possible months of stress for your child and yourself, wait until both she and you are ready. In my experience this is usually between 18 and 24 months. However, for many children and parents the time may not be quite right until much later. The important thing to remember is that it is not the child's age that is important, but whether they are showing all the right signs of being physically, emotionally and psychologically ready, and that the timing is right for you and the rest of the family.

Q My daughter now aged three years and two months was potty trained very quickly at 26 months. She has been dry every morning for the last three weeks, but at least twice a week she wakes up with a dirty nappy. I feel that we are never going to progress to getting her out of nappies totally if she keeps doing a poo in the night. None of my friends has experienced this problem, nor have I found the answer in the many baby books that cover potty training.

A When removing your daughter's nappy in the morning pay particular attention to whether the poo is very soft and comes away with the nappy or whether it is quite dry and hardened onto her bottom. This will give you an idea of whether she is actually doing a poo in the early hours of the morning or just after she wakes up.

If the poo is hardened onto her bottom it is obvious that

she is doing it in the early hours. The cause of this is often diet related; check that you are not giving her too much fruit in the late afternoon. Try giving her daily intake of fruit in the morning for a few days to see if this improves things. Also look at the time she is having her tea and last drink at night. Teatime is best around 5/5.30pm with a drink followed by their last big drink no later than 6pm.

If the poo is soft it is possible she is doing it on waking. I would therefore try getting her up slightly earlier and putting her on the potty before she manages to fill her nappy. As she gets older she should learn to get up by herself when she needs a poo, and hopefully return to bed if it is too early.

Q My son is three and a half and still has an accident three or four times a week, usually when we are visiting friends. I am starting to feel very angry when this happens as I find it embarrassing because all of my friends' children seem to have gone beyond the occasional accident stage.

A Many children of this age continue to have the odd accident and I personally would not be too worried about three or four accidents a week, particularly as it is probably because he is so engrossed in play with other children.

Normally I'm not in favour of reminding a child at this age, but I think a gentle reminder on days out would do no harm particularly if you could get the other mothers to agree to remind their children at the same time. This would avoid your son feeling like the odd one out.

While it is important that you try not to show how angry you are I think he is old enough to realise that there must be a consequence to his accident. I would chastise him but I would insist that he changed into his clean pants by himself and that he must rinse the wet pants out in the sink, before putting them in a plastic bag to take home.

Q My daughter, aged 29 months, who has been potty trained for nearly a month now, was always prone to bouts of nappy rash as a baby. I thought this would stop once she was out of nappies during the day, and although things have improved she still is prone to getting a sore red bottom every few days.

A If you are finding that her nappy is very wet in the morning it may be worthwhile trying a different brand to see if it is more absorbent. Also look at the amount of fluid that she is drinking before bedtime. I normally advise a drink of no more than 5/6oz from a cup no later than 6pm and I always delay putting the nappy on until they are about to get into bed, so that I can put them on the pot one last time just before they go to bed. If a child were shouting for more to drink I would offer them a small drink of water, but no more than a couple of ounces.

It is also worthwhile putting some cream on her bottom several times a day. There are types of homeopathic creams which contain calendula and this will help protect her skin but are not as sticky as the normal nappy rash cream.

Ensure that her bottom is cleaned and dried properly after she does a pee and a poo. Try to avoid using baby wipes, scented soap and bleached loo roll for a while, as all of these things can irritate the skin. Putting her in one hundred per cent cotton pants is also advisable, as polyester mix fabric does not allow the skin to breathe.

Q My daughter has been potty trained since she was 22 months. She is now nearly three years old and goes to the loo without being reminded, manages to pull her pants down and back up by herself and wash her own hands. However when she does a poo she always shouts for my husband or I to go and wipe her bottom. My husband says she should be able to manage this by herself now and is beginning to get quite cross when she shouts out. How can I persuade her to wipe her own bottom?

A I think she is still a little young to manage this all by herself. The majority of children do not manage to wipe themselves properly until after three years of age, most usually managing this task successfully somewhere between three and four years.

However, it is important that you spend time teaching her how to do this. Start off by guiding her hand with loo roll in it, then finish off cleaning the bits she has missed yourself. As she gets more adept at cleaning herself properly, encourage her to do it herself and say that you will come and check once she is finished.

It is important to teach little girls the importance of wiping their bottoms from front to back.

Q My son who is 26 months old has been potty trained for nearly two months and has started playing with his willy. My health visitor assured me that this behaviour was perfectly normal in little boys and just to ignore it. However, when visiting my husband's parents last weekend he was constantly rubbing and playing with it in front of everyone. My in-laws were horrified and said we must put an instant stop to 'his disgusting behaviour'. My husband has now started to get angry and shouts at our son every time he sees his hand wandering to his private parts. I'm at my wits end at how to deal with this behaviour; while I do not want my son to get a complex about his penis I do get very embarrassed when he starts to play with it.

A It is very common for both girls and boys to start examining and playing with their private parts once the nappy is abandoned. They are discovering a part of their body that up until now they did not know existed and when played with gives them pleasurable sensations. This is all part of their natural development and no child should be chastised for this behaviour. However, they must come to learn that it is something that is not done in front of other people.

With children under 28 months distraction is usually the best way to deal with this situation. When they are sitting on the potty encourage them do something with their hands like reading a book or playing with a puzzle toy.

By the time the child gets to nearer three years old the interest becomes less, but should it still persist, explain to your son that it is okay if he wants to touch his willy but it should to be done in the privacy of his own room. If you are out and about and he starts to play with himself, tell him gently and firmly that he should take a trip to the bathroom. If you adopt a special look for these situations he will soon get the hint. If he continues to play with himself excessively it would be worthwhile discussing it with your health visitor to try and discover if there is an underlying psychological reason causing this behaviour.

Potty Training in One Week

Q My son, who is eighteen months old, seems to be aware when he needs to do a pee or a poo as he will point to the potty when he is about to do one. But he is very erratic about taking instructions when it actually comes to sitting on the potty; sometimes he will sit happily for 10–15 minutes, occasionally doing a poo or pee, other times he will resist sitting on the potty and start running around all over the place.

A Your son is obviously showing signs of having some bladder control, but he is still very young and probably not ready yet either psychologically or emotionally. Do not force the issue as this could lead him to becoming quite rebellious about using the potty. I would be inclined to put the potty away for a couple of weeks, then try again with Stage One. However, do continue to take him to the toilet with you a couple of times a day, explaining simply and briefly what you are doing.

During the two weeks I would encourage him to participate in other tasks such as dressing and undressing, and helping to tidy his toys away. Although he is young, I would introduce a star chart and reward him with lots of praise and a star or sticker when he willingly co-operates. Even if he doesn't fully understand the concept of the star chart, the number of stars or stickers each day on the chart will be a good indication as to how co-operative he has been. I also find it helpful to mark a cross in the box every time I request the child to do something; if they co-operate I cover the cross with a sticker. You can then tell at a glance how many of your requests has been completed willingly.

Once you see several consecutive days where nearly all the crosses are covered with a sticker, you could bring the potty back out and try Stage One of potty training. Start off by taking him to the toilet with you again and encouraging him to sit on the potty fully clothed. If he consistently sits on the potty two to three days in a row, you can then gradually introduce the potty at night and in the morning, setting a time limit of only five minutes each time. Each time he sits on the potty for this length of time he should be given lots of praise and a sticker. Gradually increase the length of time he is expected to sit on the potty to ten minutes, but not any longer than this.

Do not go on to Stage Two of potty training until you are confident that he is happily and consistently following the instructions in Stage One, and that you are also ready to devote the time required to potty train him in a week.

Q My daughter is nearly two years of age and has been potty trained for nearly three months. However she still has the occasional accident two or three times a week. How should I deal with this? Am I being unrealistic that she should be aware whenever she needs to go to the loo?

A Your daughter potty trained at a very young age and occasional accidents are to be expected. It would be worthwhile keeping a chart for a few days to see if there is a pattern to her accidents. It is often when a child is engrossed in play or becomes over-tired. If you can pin-point when the accidents are happening then you can give her gentle reminders at these times.

However, it is important to remember not to go back to reminding her all the time, only at the times accidents are most likely to occur.

It is also important not to scold her when she has an accident, but it is worthwhile drawing her attention again to the difference between wet and dry and how much nicer it is to wear nice clean pants. When she does have an accident I think it is important that she is made to change into her dry pants herself, so that she understands the consequence of wetting her pants.

Q My son is nearly 20 months and will happily sit on the potty twice a day for five to ten minutes. However, as yet he had never actually done anything in the potty. Should I continue to sit him on the potty or abandon things for a while?

A I would continue to sit him on the potty for these two short spells and give him lots of praise for sitting so nicely, as long as he is happy to do so. However, as he is still very young I would abandon it if he begins to show signs of rebellion and boredom. If this happens put the potty away and try again in two or three weeks.

Should he continue to sit happily I would continue to put him on the pot twice a day and take him to the loo with you two or three times a day, following the advice on page 31 at the preparation stage of pottying.

The aim at this stage is that he is happy to sit on the potty for short spells and also happy to obey simple instructions. These things are actually more important at this stage as it will help the potty training procedure work more quickly once he does start to pee in the potty.

Q Should I encourage my son to help me empty and clean the potty after he has used it?

A I usually find that within a very short time of being potty trained most children are happy to use the loo more often than the potty. For that reason I do not make a big deal of actually encouraging them to help empty and clean the potty. However, if they were insistent on helping I would allow them to, but on the agreement we do it together. This helps avoid extra work of cleaning up the spills that are likely to occur if the child attempts the task by himself.

If your child is determined to help empty and clean the potty it would be advisable to keep all cleaning agents out of reach. One mother I know used to allow her son to spray the anti-bacterial cleanser into the potty. Then one day he got hold of the spray before she could stop him and attempted to spray it into the potty; unfortunately the nozzle was facing the wrong way and he sprayed it into his eyes. He had to be rushed to hospital and kept in overnight for observation. Fortunately there was no long-term damage, but it was still a frightening experience for the child and his parents.

If your child is insistent on helping empty and clean the potty I would advise that it should only be rinsed out with cold water when he is helping, and disinfected at a later stage.

Further Reading

Also available from Vermilion by Gina Ford

The prices shown above are correct at time of going to press. However, the publishers reserve the right to increase prices on covers from those previously advertised, without further notice.

FREE POSTAGE AND PACKING
Overseas customers allow £2.00 per paperback

BY PHONE: 01624 677237

BY POST: Random House Books
C/o Bookpost, PO Box 29, Douglas
Isle of Man, IM99 1BQ

BY FAX: 01624 670923

BY EMAIL: bookshop@enterprise.net

Checques (payable to Bookpost) and credit cards accepted

Prices and availability subject to change without notice.
Allow 28 days for delivery.
When placing your order, please mention if you do not wish to receive any additional information.

www.randomhouse.co.uk